LET'S PLAY! LITTLE CHAMPS

SKATEBOARDING

KIM THOMPSON

NorwoodHouse Press

Cataloging-in-Publication Data

Names: Thompson, Kim, 1970-.
Title: Skateboarding / Kim Thompson.
Description: Buffalo, NY : Norwood House Press, 2026. | Series: Let's play! little champs | Includes glossary and index.
Identifiers: ISBN 9781978577251 (pbk.) | ISBN 9781978577268 (library bound) | ISBN 9781978577275 (ebook)
Subjects: LCSH: Skateboarding--Juvenile literature.
Classification: LCC GV859.8 T474 2026 | DDC 796.22--dc23

Published in 2026 by
Norwood House Press
2544 Clinton Street
Buffalo, NY 14224

Designer: Rhea Magaro

Photo credits: Cover, pp. 1, 12 kornnphoto/Shutterstock.com; p. 5 Ally Foster/Shutterstock.com; p. 6 travelview/Shutterstock.com; p. 7 Uryupina Nadezhda/Shutterstock.com; p. 9 LadyRhino/Shutterstock.com; p. 10 Lazy_Bear/Shutterstock.com; p. 11 Yankovsky88/Shutterstock.com; p. 14 Arlette Lopez/Shutterstock.com; p. 15 paulzhuk/Shutterstock.com; p. 16 Filip Jedraszak/Shutterstock.com; p. 17 Guillermo Spelucin R/Shutterstock.com; p. 18 Flystock/Shutterstock.com; p. 19 lzf/Shutterstock.com; p. 21 ADDICTIVE STOCK/Shutterstock.com

Printed in the United States of America

CPSIA compliance information: Batch #CWNHP26: For further information contact Norwood House Press at 1-800-237-9932.

TABLE OF CONTENTS

What Is Skateboarding?

Skateboarding is a fun sport. It was invented by surfers who wanted to practice their moves on land.

Skateboarders ride on boards with wheels. They learn to do amazing tricks!

Skateboarding is a full-body workout. It builds strong muscles. It teaches **balance** and **coordination**.

As they practice tricks, skateboarders also learn patience and **persistence**!

The Gear

Skateboards have three main parts: the deck, trucks, and wheels. The deck is a long, narrow board that may be made of wood. Metal **trucks** connect the board to the wheels. This allows the rider to turn.

Shoes protect the rider's feet. They must stick to the board. Flat, rubber-bottomed sneakers are good choices.

Some riders put grip tape on their boards to improve **traction** and keep their feet in place.

Skateboarders fall a lot! Wearing safety gear is very important.

Riders need a skateboarding helmet. They need knee and elbow pads. Wrist guards provide even more protection.

Where to Ride

Beginners learn to ride on flat surfaces such as driveways or bike paths.

A **skate park** has many fun challenges for riders. There are ramps, rails, and **half-pipes**. Curved **bowls** are great for building speed and doing tricks in the air.

Skateboarding Tricks

Skateboarders learn to do hundreds of tricks. They invent more all the time!

To do an ollie, the rider pops the back of the board off the ground. The skater gets a ride as the board flies through the air.

For a kickflip, the rider jumps and kicks the board to flip it in the air. They catch the board before landing.

For grinds, riders jump up and slide the skateboard along a rail or ledge.

How to Be Skateboard-Ready

Skateboarders should eat healthy foods like fruits, vegetables, and lean meats. They should drink plenty of water. Getting enough sleep keeps them alert and ready to ride.

GLOSSARY

balance (BAL-uhns): the ability to stay steady and not fall over

bowls (bohlz): curved areas in skate parks that look like big empty swimming pools where skateboarders can ride up and down the sides

coordination (koh-or-duh-NAY-shuhn): the ability to make different parts of your body work together smoothly

half-pipes (HAF-pipes): u-shaped ramps that allow skateboarders to ride up and down the curved walls and do tricks at the top

persistence (pur-SIS-tuhns): the ability to keep trying even when something is hard or when you make mistakes

skate park (skayt park): a special place built for skateboarding with ramps, rails, and other fun things to ride on

traction (TRAK-shuhn): the force that keeps a moving body from slipping on a surface

trucks (truhks): the metal parts that connect the skateboard wheels to the bottom of the board and that can be tightened or loosened for different tricks

THINKING QUESTIONS

1. Who invented skateboarding?
2. What are the three main parts of a skateboard?
3. Why is safety gear especially important for skateboarders?
4. What safety gear do skateboarders need?
5. How do you do an ollie?

INDEX

ABOUT THE AUTHOR

Kim Thompson is a writer, mom, and sports fan from Columbus, Ohio. She loves to watch athletes' amazing skills on the court, field, or diamond. She believes that all kids should try out the sports that interest them and always remember to have fun!